Made in the USA
Columbia, SC
10 May 2022

60221395R00067